To

_____

From

_____

"Like roses, children thrive on love."

A tribute to my mother

_____

_____

_____

_____

_____

_____

_____

_____

_____

_____

_____

_____

_____

Heartstrings

OF LAUGHTER AND LOVE

A TRIBUTE TO

Mothers

J

COUNTRYMAN

When I think of the essence of my mother's life, I remember the winter of my sixth year.

Dad was going to college and, with four school-age children to feed, money was scarce. Dreading the thought of four empty stockings on Christmas morning, Dad decided he would get a job at night to earn extra money. Mom knew this would cut into his precious study time just when final papers and exams were approaching, so she suggested an alternate plan—she would try selling her sweet rolls.

For the next several weeks, while we were at school each day, she made dozens of wonderful sweet rolls, smothered in a creamy, white sugar-glaze with nuts and cherry and pineapple fillings oozing over the sides. As soon as we got home from school she would hand us packages of warm rolls wrapped in foil to sell to the neighbors. It was terribly cold so we tucked the rolls into our coats to keep warm. I was afraid to go up to the doors at first, but when the neighbors began praising the delectable sweet rolls and buying all our packages with orders for more, my courage increased. Soon I was striding happily up and down the campus streets, proud to be selling my mother's confections—proud that we were helping my father earn high marks on his studies.

This little incident is a cameo of my mother's life— one of resourcefulness, determination, and a deep, abiding love for her family. She has always been happiest when giving and doing for others. What a great treasure that this mother should be mine!

This book is dedicated to all beloved mothers. It is a collection —gifts of gratitude to our mothers for the love we can never truly repay.

May God bless and reward our dear mothers,
both here on earth and in heaven.

Terri Gibbs

EDITOR

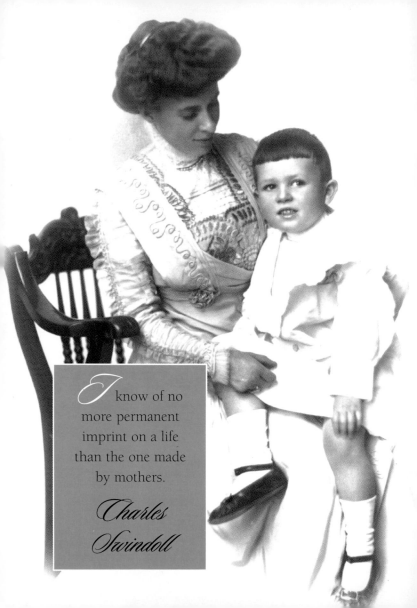

I know of no
more permanent
imprint on a life
than the one made
by mothers.

*Charles
Swindoll*

The process of shaping the child . . . shapes also the mother herself. Reverence for her sacred burden calls her to all that is pure and good, that she may teach primarily by her own humble, daily example.

Elisabeth Elliot

THE SHAPING OF A CHRISTIAN FAMILY

A Potpourri for Mother

To a basin of dried scented roses add a handful of dried knotted Marjoram, lemon thyme, Rosemary, Lavender flowers all well dried, the rind of one lemon and one orange dried to powder, six dried bay leaves, half an ounce of bruised cloves, a teaspoon of Allspice. Mix well together and stir occasionally.

Dated 1895

BY ANY OTHER NAME

Love begins by taking care of the closest ones—the ones at home.

Mother Teresa

Dear Mother,

Thank you for the example you have been to me. You may be only 4 feet 7 inches tall, but in my eyes you have always stood tall.

From my early childhood I can remember how our home was always open to anyone and everyone who needed food, fellowship, or fun! We played many silly games with anyone who expressed the slightest interest. I remember how you would fix homemade cream puffs every Friday night for all the kids in the neighborhood. No wonder the kids all loved to come to our house!

I recall those years in Alaska when we would move all of our furniture to set up tables for holiday meals so all the military boys and families who were away from relatives could come to our home.

In sixty-one years of marriage and ministry, you and Daddy have given of yourselves unselfishly. At times I wonder how you've been able to do so much all these years . . . surely it is through God's grace. Only eternity will reveal the lives you have touched by the love you have always shown to others. Your example has taught me to love others also. I am so grateful that you are my mother!

Mary McGee

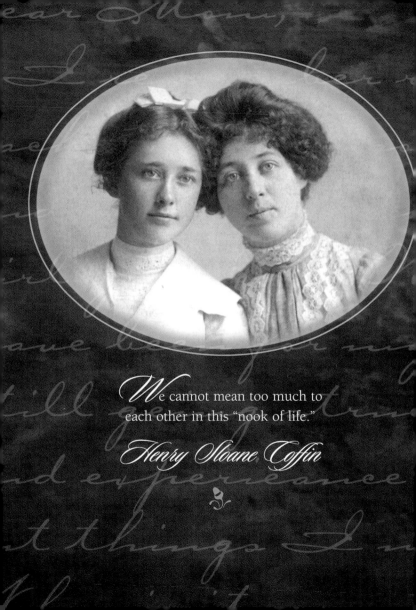

We cannot mean too much to
each other in this "nook of life."

Henry Sloane Coffin

$\mathcal{M}$y father's salary was very small, so there were economies of every kind. Mother had learned to sew by a Singer Sewing Machine company correspondence course, and she did ingenious things with fabric bought on sale—remnants. . . . Her cooking of necessity had to be simple, but she gave things a twist as to flavor and beauty. When I wanted to earn money by starting a candy business, many long hours she helped me to make fudge and penuche and coconut bars, until she got neuritis in her shoulder from doing so much hand beating. We made the magnificent sum of seventy dollars from our combined efforts.

Edith Schaeffer

THE TAPESTRY

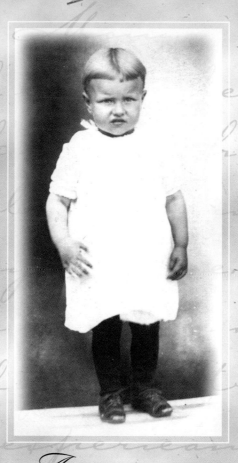

*A*ll that is purest and best
in man is but the echo of
a mother's benediction.

Frederick W. Morton

Duty makes us do things well, but love makes us do them beautifully.

Phillips Brooks

A mother is completely fatigued. She has been telling her friends for weeks that there is nothing left of her, and then a child falls ill and needs her. Week after week, by night and day, she stands by and never thinks of being tired.

Harry Emerson Fosdick

Dear Mom,

You have a love that is all-encompassing, never fading, ever-expanding — your devotion and tenderness are the closest thing I know to the infinite love of God.

Luke Gibbs

"*Lying there after her ordeal, with the baby on her arm, she knew the age-old surge of mother-love. All her old love of life seemed to concentrate on one thing—the little soft, helpless bundle.*"

Bess Streeter Aldrich

The most glorious sight that one ever sees beneath the stars is the sight of worthy motherhood.

George W. Truett

My mother, whose disposition was always bright and optimistic, was active, energetic and wholly devoted to her large family. No sacrifice was too great, no task too hard, for her willing heart and hands. Her work was hard and her hours long. Only God knows the number of nights she walked the floor, rocked the cradle, or sat by the bedside of her children during their many, many ailments.

Oswald J. Smith
THE STORY OF MY LIFE

A true mother is not merely a provider, house-keeper, comforter, or companion. A true mother is primarily and essentially a trainer.

Ruth Bell Graham

It's difficult to know what counts in this world. Most of us count credits, honor, dollars. But at the bulging center of mid-life, I am beginning to see that the things that really matter take place not in the boardrooms, but in the kitchens of the world. Memory, imagination, love are some of those things. Service to God and the ones we love is another.

Gary Allen Sledge

(READER'S DIGEST, SEPTEMBER 1989)

Slipping on Mother's old apron is like getting a big hug from her.

Joyce Smit

In my childhood home, we would spend an hour at the table after we had eaten, talking or reading Bible story books. I don't recall the little ones fussing. Mother would hold the baby and Father would hold the next and I'd hold the next. There was real togetherness.

Ingrid Trobisch

"Under the elm tree stood a pretty tea table, covered with bread and butter, custards and berries, and in the middle a fine cake with sugar-roses on the top; and mamma and baby, all nicely dressed, were waiting to welcome them to the birthday feast."

Louisa May Alcott

SHADOW CHILDREN

*W*omen like to make sacrifices in one big piece, to give God something grand, but we can't. Our lives are a mosaic of little things, like putting a rose in a vase on the table.

Ingrid Trobisch

Dear Momma,

*H*ow can I thank you for all you taught me? Your love of life, music, and family will always be interwoven into my person. I will never forget the hundreds of times you played the piano while Sissy and I danced our own terrible ballet.

Now that you are gone, I realize the music of your life still plays in my life— and that it doesn't matter how I dance, just as long as I do.

Your daughter,

Jana Muntsinger

*G*od could not be everywhere, and therefore He made mothers.

Jewish Proverb

A Tribute to Our Beloved Mum, Myrtle Ivy McMartin, from Her Daughters

*O*ur mother's life drew together so many Christlike characteristics that the Bible praises and the world desperately needs. Always manifesting unruffled strength and gentleness, her love for God and her faith in God were unshakable. Mum trusted God for each one of her children. She prayed for us, believed in us, and loved all of us unconditionally. We are fulfilling our God-given destinies because our mother dedicated her life to bringing us up in the way of the Lord. As a grandma she somehow planted herself forever in each grandchild's young heart. She has finished her time here on earth, but her influence keeps flowing on down through her children and her grandchildren. One can only imagine the beauty of our mum as she worships around the eternal throne.

We love you Mum,

Jean, Lynne, and Ruth

(New South Wales, Australia)

No man is poor who had a godly mother.

Abraham Lincoln

When I was a boy, my mother and I would make eye contact, and she would give me a smile that would make my day. Her eyes and her smile would say, "I love you, you're terrific." She was the center of my universe, and, like most children, I thought I had the most wonderful mother in the world. I adored her.

Bob Keeshan

(CAPTAIN KANGAROO)

Parents who care unselfishly for their children, who provide for them spiritually as well as materially, are performing an invaluable service. They are helping to create a stable and secure world.

Robert McCracken

❧

A mother can read all the child-rearing books and can subscribe to any theory of parenting, but what gets passed along to her children is something far more intimate and mysterious than anything contained therein. What gets passed along is her character, and it enters into her kids as surely and as inexorably as water flows from a fuller vessel into a less-full one.

Laurence Shames

❧

"The nursery was a big room, and in the evening a bright wood-fire always burned there for baby. Mamma sat before it softly rubbing baby's little rosy limbs before she went to bed, singing and telling stories meanwhile to the three children who pranced about in their long nightgowns."

Louisa May Alcott
"SHADOW CHILDREN"

I am not in any doubt as to how my own Christian experience began. The altar before which I knelt first was my mother's knee.

L. D. Weatherhead

My mother was a striking beauty who left the world a more beautiful place than she found it. She grew lovely flowers, did the finest needlepoint I have ever seen, and knew how to keep an exquisite home. . . .

She taught me a great deal, although neither of us realized it at the time. Probably her most important lesson was an inadvertent one.

You have two choices in life: You can like what you do, or you can dislike it. I have chosen to like it.

Barbara Bush

A MEMOIR

Many women have done
excellently, but you surpass them all.

Proverbs 31:29

To Mother

You painted no Madonnas
On chapel walls in Rome,
But with a touch diviner
You lived one in your home. . . .

You built no great cathedrals
That centuries applaud
But with a grace exquisite
Your life cathedraled God. . . .

T. W. Fessenden

Dear Louy [Louisa May Alcott],

I am glad you put your heart in the right place;
for I am sure all true strength comes from above.
Continue to feel that God is near you, dear child, and
He never will forsake you in a weak moment. Write
me always when you feel that I can help you;
for, though God is near, Mother never forgets you,
and your refuge is her arms. . . .
Mother

Louisa May Alcott

LIFE, LETTERS, AND JOURNALS

A mother's days are made wearisome by the wants and frequent waywardness of little children, and her nights are often made wakeful by their illnesses. But while those little ones are burdens, they are such lovable bundles of graceful curves and such constant sources of surprise and joy.

Ralph Sockman

*Beautiful faces are those that wear
Whole-souled honesty printed there.*

Ellen Palmer Allerton

I am eternally grateful to my
mother for many things, but one
of the most enduring blessings she
brought into my life was to teach me
the Catechism at the age of ten that
"God is a Spirit, infinite, eternal, and
unchangeable in His being, wisdom,
power, holiness, justice, goodness, and
truth." That definition of God has been
with me all my life, and when a man
knows in his heart that God is an
infinite, eternal, and unchangeable
Spirit, it helps to overcome the
temptation to limit Him.

Billy Graham
PEACE WITH GOD

If I knocked on my mother's door, she always answered; and if I entered [her writing room] . . ., she never seemed to mind. She would put down her pen immediately and smile gently and ask what I wanted. . . . As she turned toward the doorway, with the light from the window on her face, I could tell she was very glad to see me.

Reeve
Lindbergh
(DAUGHTER OF ANNE MORROW LINDBERGH)

In all the little daily patterns of the home—the laundry going into the same hamper, the sweaters into the same drawer, the hair getting washed and the shoes polished on Saturday nights—God is at work.

He delights to glorify Himself in the commonplace. . . . He makes our little daily chores channels of His grace.

Anne Ortlund

The great doing of little things makes the great life.

Eugenia Price

My Mother

Who fed me from her gentle breast
And hushed me in her arms to rest,
And on my cheek sweet kisses prest?
My mother.

Who taught my infant
lips to pray,
To love God's holy word
and day,
And walk in wisdom's
pleasant way? My mother.

And can I ever cease to be
Affectionate and kind to thee
Who wast so very kind to
me,—My mother.

Oh no, the thought I
cannot bear;
And if God please my
life to spare
I hope I shall reward thy care,
My mother. . . .

Jane Taylor

1783-1824

Mothers, You Are Great!

I know of no more permanent imprint on a life than the one made by mothers. I guess that's why Mother's Day always leaves me a little nostalgic. Not simply because my mother has gone on (and heaven's probably cleaner because of it!), but because that's the one day the real heroines of our world get the credit they deserve. Hats off to every one of you!

More than any statesman or teacher, more than any minister or physician, more than any film star, athlete, business person, author, scientist, civic leader, entertainer, or military hero . . . you are the most influential person in your child's life.

Never doubt that fact.

Not even when the dishes in the sink resemble the Leaning Tower . . . or the washing machine gets choked and dies . . . or the place looks a wreck and nobody at home stops to say, "Thanks Mom. You're great."

It's still worth it. You *are* great. This is your time to make the most significant contribution in all of life. Don't sell it short. In only a few years it will all be a memory. Make it a good one.

Charles Swindoll

THE FINISHING TOUCH

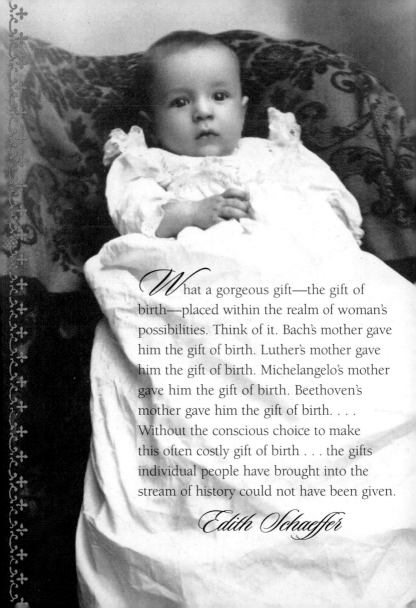

*W*hat a gorgeous gift—the gift of birth—placed within the realm of woman's possibilities. Think of it. Bach's mother gave him the gift of birth. Luther's mother gave him the gift of birth. Michelangelo's mother gave him the gift of birth. Beethoven's mother gave him the gift of birth. . . . Without the conscious choice to make this often costly gift of birth . . . the gifts individual people have brought into the stream of history could not have been given.

Edith Schaeffer

I made it a rule to take my children one at a time into my room; and having been careful to see that they were comfortably seated . . . I would say, "I'm going to talk to Jesus," and then before my child, would pour out my soul to Him. Oh, how precious are the memories of little pinafores lifted to wipe my eyes or the sound of sweet little voices saying, "Don't cry, Mother."

Amelia Hudson Broomhall

1 8 7 5

T he heart of a mother is a deep abyss at the bottom of which you will always discover forgiveness.

Honore de Balzac

A TEATIME BLESSING

*L*ord, grant that our time together
be steeped in serenity, sweetened by
sharing, and surrounded by the warm
fragrance of your love.

Amen

Emilie Barnes

IF TEACUPS COULD TALK

What a treat to have tea with Mother. Along with a pot of steaming tea, cream, and sugar, serve these wonderfully fluffy biscuits (scones) piping hot from the oven. Smother in butter and top with fresh strawberry preserves and whipped cream. Of course you will want to serve it all in your best china on starched white linen with a lovely bouquet of flowers or some forced winter blossoms.

BUTTERMILK BISCUITS (Scones)

3 cups sifted flour
1 teaspoon salt
1 1/2 teaspoons baking soda
1 teaspoon cream of tartar
2/3 cup shortening
1 1/4 cups buttermilk

Preheat the oven to 450 F.°

Sift the dry ingredients into a bowl. Add the shortening and blend together with a pastry cutter until the mixture resembles cornmeal. Add the buttermilk and stir well.

Place the dough mixture on a lightly floured work surface. Knead the dough lightly just for a minute, being careful not to add too much flour. Roll out to 1/2 inch thickness. Cut the dough into 3-4 inch circles close to each other. Place the circles 1/2 inch apart on a sturdy baking sheet and bake in a preheated 450° oven for 13 minutes.

This recipe yields one dozen large, scrumptious biscuits (scones).

I understood . . . the value of having a mother who had not stopped taking chances and looking at life with delight. It was comforting to know that I was not at the head of the parade, that there was an older, wiser woman moving in front of me.

Phyllis Theroux

*N*ext to God we are indebted to women, first for life itself, and then for making it worth having.

Bovée

*T*hou art thy mother's glass,
and she in thee
calls back the lovely April
of her prime.

William Shakespeare

A kind face is a
beautiful face.

Anonymous

There is no love on earth, I think, as potent and enduring as a mother's love for her child.

Ann Kiemel Anderson

I associate childhood prayers with bedtime and warm milk, with a turned-down lamp or flickering candle, and with the reassuring presence of my mother as we faced the adventure of another night.

The routine of prayer was snuggled somewhere between the protests or the tired acceptance of bed, and the giggles and squabbles that would follow until sleep came.

David H. C. Read

(pastor for many years of Madison Avenue
Presbyterian Church in New York City)

THIS GRACE GIVEN

*N*o nation ever had a better friend than the mother who taught her children to pray.

Anonymous

When Peter got home his mother forgave him,
because she was so glad to see that he had found his
shoes and coat. Cotton-tail and Peter folded up the
pocket-handkerchief, and old Mrs. Rabbit strung up the
onions and hung them from the kitchen ceiling, with
the bunches of herbs."

Beatrix Potter

A Tribute to Edith Gibbs from Her Six Children

As a girl you helped your parents make their prairie farm a home.

As a teenager you left that home to work alone in the city and attend high school.

As a young woman you became one of the few women of your time to earn a college degree.

As a wife you made the parsonage a cosy haven, living a life of loving sacrifice.

As a widow you overcame your grief to raise six children alone, teaching English at high school and love at home.

As a grandmother you never forget a birthday or miss an opportunity to pray.

We thank you, Mom, for your godly example of motherhood—it is our invaluable legacy and that of our children and their children.

We love you Mom,

Jim, David, Marylee, Carl, Bill, and Gwen

Mother—that was the bank where we deposited all our hurts and worries.

T. DeWitt Talmage

Mother's Prima Ballerina

*I*n my memory, my childhood years form a mellow hodgepodge of love, joy, and the thrill of conquering new challenges.

I was definitely a tomboy, but somehow my mother persuaded me to take ballet lessons, and I've always been grateful for that. The teacher was a woman from Russia who had moved to the area for some reason, and she was a very strict, very disciplined instructor. She taught lessons once a week in the American Legion Hall, and her mother would come along to play the piano for us while we danced. My mother sewed all my costumes for the recitals, of course—elaborate sequined-and-feathered outfits that seem just as enchanting today in the old photographs as they did so many years ago. After the Russian teacher moved away, Mom drove me to Angelton, a town about twenty miles away, so I could continue dance lessons with Ruth and Sara Munson, two sisters from West Columbia.

Ruth Ryan

(wife of Nolan Ryan)

COVERING HOME

A Mother's Birthday

Lord Jesus, Thou has known
    A mother's love and tender care:
    And thou wilt hear,
    While for my own
    Mother most dear
    I make this birthday prayer.
Protect her life, I pray,
    who gave the gift of life to me;
    And may she know,
    From day to day,
    The deepening glow
    of joy that comes from Thee. . . .
Ah, hold her by the hand,
    As once her hand held mine;
    And though she may
    Not understand
    Life's winding way,
    Lead her in peace divine.
I cannot pay my debt
    For all the love that she has given;
    But Thou, love's Lord,
    Wilt not forget
    Her due reward,—
    Bless her in earth and heaven.

HENRY VAN DYKE

1852-1933

A Tribute to My Mom, Jeannine Sawyer of Brownwood, Texas

As a single mom in the '50s, with three young children and no education, my mom faced many challenges. She worked long, hard hours in a non-air-conditioned woolen mill for little pay. The amazing thing was her optimistic attitude. I remember how excited she was when she was able to get us a place to live in a government-subsidized housing project. It was cheap, but it was clean.

At first we had very little furniture, not even a table for the kitchen.

This didn't bother Mom. For our first meal, she fixed us hot dogs, and we sat on the floor on a blanket. She said, "Isn't this great! We're having a picnic in our very own kitchen." She made the situation seem like fun. We laughed and joked and had a great time. Much later I realized what a true marvel she was. Instead of feeling down and beleaguered, she embraced the good in life and taught us to do the same.

How grateful I am for the example she set.

Karen Griffin

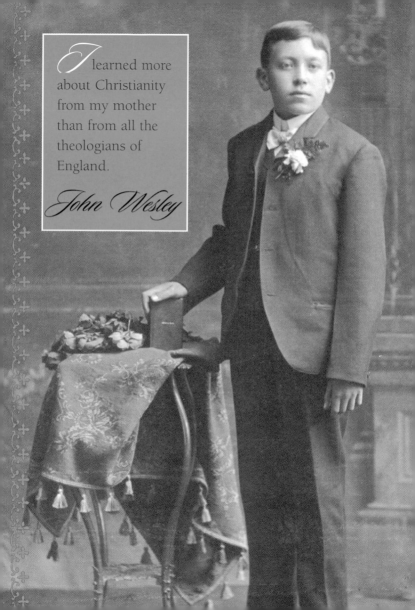

I learned more about Christianity from my mother than from all the theologians of England.

John Wesley

When I was a young man, I had plenty of people to wipe away my tears. I had two big sisters who put me under their wings. I had a dozen or so aunts and uncles. I had a mother who worked nights as a nurse and days as a mother—excercising both professions with tenderness. . . .

My mother still lives in the same house. You couldn't pay her to move. The house that seemed so big when I was a boy now feels tiny. On the wall are pictures of Mom in her youth—her hair autumn-brown, her face irresistibly beautiful. I see her now—still healthy, still vivacious, but with wrinkles, graying hair, slower step. Would that I could wave the wand and make everything new again. Would that I could put her once again in the strong embrace of the high-plains cowboy she loved and buried. Would that I could stretch out the wrinkles and take off the bifocals and restore the spring to her step, would that I could make everything new. . . but I can't.

Max Lucado

THE APPLAUSE OF HEAVEN

House and Home

A house is built of logs and stone,
of tiles and posts and piers;
A home is built of loving deeds
That stand a thousand years.

Victor Hugo

*E*very mother practices the ritual of
counting tiny fingers and toes, cupping
the small head in one's hand, stroking
gossamer hair, and trying to determine
just whose side of the family is respon-
sible for those ears and that nose—all
rites of new motherhood, both private
and public, that mark the beginning of
a whole new world.

Pamela Scurry
CRADLE AND ALL

 have been told that my mother, when she surmised from the face of the physician that her life and that of her child could not both be saved, begged him to spare the child. . . . So through these many years of mine, I have seldom thanked God for His mercies without thanking Him for my mother.

James M. Ludlow 1919

My Altar

The things in life that are worthy
Were born in my mother's breast
And breathed into mine by the magic
Of the love her life expressed.
The years that have
brought me to manhood
Have taken her far from me;
But memory keeps me from straying
Too far from my mother's knee.

John H. Styles, Jr.

Three Cheers for Mother!

Over the centuries she's worked as hard as father and for very different reasons.

He has built the houses; she's added the colors, the smells, the music.

He has shaped constitutions to make citizens protected; she has sewn flags to make them weep and cheer.

He has mustered armies and police forces to put down oppression; she has prayed for them and patted them on the back and sent them off with their heads up.

He has shaped decisions; she has added morale.

Celebrate the mother! She, too, no less than the father, has, under God, shaped a magnificent human tradition.

Anne Ortlund

DISCIPLINES OF THE HOME

A mother's arms are made of tenderness, and children sleep soundly in them.

Victor Hugo

A mother is a chalice, the vessel without which no human being has ever been born. She is created to be a life-bearer, cooperating with her husband and with God in the making of a child. What a solemn responsibility. What an unspeakable privilege—a vessel divinely prepared for the Master's use.

Elisabeth Elliot

Dear Mom,

I can still smell the freshly baked cookies and taste the big glass of cold milk that were always on the table waiting for me when I arrived home from a busy day at school. You were synonymous with June Cleaver on "Leave It to Beaver." You were always home when I got there. You made sure I had a fresh scrubbed look at all times, glistening hair, and a starched dress. You saw to it that I had music lessons the first twenty years of my life, which taught me great self-discipline.

I look at you now with advanced Alzheimer's disease and realize you are gone. Once in a great while a spark of how you were in the past glows; your dry sense of humor breaks through the barrier, and it is amazing how you can still pray and talk about heavenly things. You are not my mother any longer but only the outer shell of what once was. My hope for you is that somewhere in your mind once in a while circuits connect and you, if only for a second, realize that you are loved.

Marci Isaacs

$\mathcal{W}$omen are aristocrats, and it is always the mother who makes us feel that we belong to the better sort.

John Lancaster Spalding

I still remember vividly the desperate, empty feeling I had in third grade on that one and only time when I came home after school to face a locked front door. My mother wasn't home! It had never happened before. There I stood paralyzed with fear, alone and crying.

Fortunately my despair was brief; Mom drove up in just a few minutes. Her welcome hug flooded over me and I felt secure again. All was well in my world. Today I'm thankful that my mom's hug still brings warmth and relief. Moms are good at that!

Lynn Rose

As long as we lived in Philadelphia, we actually walked all the way home for lunch every day. We liked to. When we burst in the door there was Mother, and there was the hot soup. It was nice to smell the soup, and it was nice that Mother was always there for us. Always.

Elisabeth Elliot

THE SHAPING OF A CHRISTIAN FAMILY

I have no greater joy than to hear that my children walk in truth.

3 John 1:4

Mother always smelled beautiful. I remember burrowing into her neck just for the soft loveliness of scented skin. After smell came sound, the sound of her voice, singing to me, talking. I took the beauty of her voice for granted until I was almost grown up.

Madeleine L'Engle

THE SUMMER OF THE GREAT GRANDMOTHER

I love old mothers—mothers with white hair, and kindly eyes, and lips grown softly sweet with murmured blessings over sleeping babes.

Charles S. Ross

*W*ith all the things we work for, or dream of having, who would ever guess that the biggest thrill of all the thrills there are is simply your child.

"Mrs. Hornstein"

FREDRICA WAGMAN